So you think you're a

HOMOPHOBE

Keep making a difference

All the best

Sophie Cook x

Sophie Cook

☆

"Bigotry, prejudice and hate are all symptoms of the same condition. It's a deficiency of the human soul. It's the deficiency of empathy. These behaviours might be motivated by feelings of superiority but they reveal a deeper inferiority and failing."

Equal Together

Sophie Cook

@sophiecooktalks

HI, I'M GARY
AND OVER THE
COMING PAGES
I WILL GIVE YOU
A LITTLE ADVICE
ABOUT YOUR
HOMOPHOBIA

Don't be a dick to other people. Don't be a dick to other people. Don't be a dick to other people. Don't be a dick to other people. Don't be a dick to other people. Don't be a dick to other people. Don't be a dick to other people. Don't be a dick to other people. Don't be a dick to other people. Don't be a dick to other people. Don't be a dick to other people. Don't be a dick to other people. Don't be a dick to other people. Don't be a dick to other people. Don't be a dick to other people. Don't be a dick

to other people. Don't be a
dick to other people. Don't
be a dick to other people.
Don't be a dick to other
people. Don't be a dick to
other people. Don't be a
dick to other people. Don't
be a dick to other people.
Don't be a dick to other
people. Don't be a dick to
other people. Don't be a
dick to other people. Don't
be a dick to other people.
Don't be a dick to other
people. Don't be a dick
to other people. Don't be
a dick to other people.
Don't be a dick to other

people. Don't be a dick to other people. Don't be a dick to other people. Don't be a dick to other people. Don't be a dick to other people. Don't be a dick to other people. Don't be a dick to other people. Don't be a dick to other people. Don't be a dick to other people. Don't be a dick to other people. Don't be a dick to other people. Don't be a dick to other people. Don't be a dick to other people. Don't be a dick to other people. Don't be a dick to other people.

Don't be a dick to other people. Don't be a dick to other people. Don't be a dick to other people. Don't be a dick to other people. Don't be a dick to other people. Don't be a dick to other people. Don't be a dick to other people. Don't be a dick to other people. Don't be a dick to other people. Don't be a dick to other people. Don't be a dick to other people. Don't be a dick to other people. Don't be a dick to other people. Don't be a dick to other people. Don't be a dick to other people. Don't be a dick

to other people. Don't be a
dick to other people. Don't
be a dick to other people.
Don't be a dick to other
people. Don't be a dick to
other people. Don't be a
dick to other people. Don't
be a dick to other people.
Don't be a dick to other
people. Don't be a dick to
other people. Don't be a
dick to other people. Don't
be a dick to other people.
Don't be a dick to other
people. Don't be a dick
to other people. Don't be
a dick to other people.
Don't be a dick to other

people. Don't be a dick to other people. Don't be a dick to other people. Don't be a dick to other people. Don't be a dick to other people. Don't be a dick to other people. Don't be a dick to other people. Don't be a dick to other people. Don't be a dick to other people. Don't be a dick to other people. Don't be a dick to other people. Don't be a dick to other people. Don't be a dick to other people. Don't be a dick to other people. Don't be a dick to other people. Don't be a dick to other people. Don't be a dick to other people.

Don't be a dick to other people. Don't be a dick to other people. Don't be a dick to other people. Don't be a dick to other people. Don't be a dick to other people. Don't be a dick to other people. Don't be a dick to other people. Don't be a dick to other people. Don't be a dick to other people. Don't be a dick to other people. Don't be a dick to other people. Don't be a dick to other people. Don't be a dick to other people. Don't be a dick to other people. Don't be a dick to other people. Don't be a dick

to other people. Don't be a
dick to other people. Don't
be a dick to other people.
Don't be a dick to other
people. Don't be a dick to
other people. Don't be a
dick to other people. Don't
be a dick to other people.
Don't be a dick to other
people. Don't be a dick to
other people. Don't be a
dick to other people. Don't
be a dick to other people.
Don't be a dick to other
people. Don't be a dick
to other people. Don't be
a dick to other people.
Don't be a dick to other

people. Don't be a dick to other people. Don't be a dick to other people. Don't be a dick to other people. Don't be a dick to other people. Don't be a dick to other people. Don't be a dick to other people. Don't be a dick to other people. Don't be a dick to other people. Don't be a dick to other people. Don't be a dick to other people. Don't be a dick to other people. Don't be a dick to other people. Don't be a dick to other people. Don't be a dick to other people. Don't be a dick to other people. Don't be a dick to other people.

Don't be a dick to other people. Don't be a dick to other people. Don't be a dick to other people. Don't be a dick to other people. Don't be a dick to other people. Don't be a dick to other people. Don't be a dick to other people. Don't be a dick to other people. Don't be a dick to other people. Don't be a dick to other people. Don't be a dick to other people. Don't be a dick to other people. Don't be a dick to other people. Don't be a dick to other people. Don't be a dick

to other people. Don't be a
dick to other people. Don't
be a dick to other people.
Don't be a dick to other
people. Don't be a dick to
other people. Don't be a
dick to other people. Don't
be a dick to other people.
Don't be a dick to other
people. Don't be a dick to
other people. Don't be a
dick to other people. Don't
be a dick to other people.
Don't be a dick to other
people. Don't be a dick
to other people. Don't be
a dick to other people.
Don't be a dick to other

people. Don't be a dick to other people. Don't be a dick to other people. Don't be a dick to other people. Don't be a dick to other people. Don't be a dick to other people. Don't be a dick to other people. Don't be a dick to other people. Don't be a dick to other people. Don't be a dick to other people. Don't be a dick to other people. Don't be a dick to other people. Don't be a dick to other people. Don't be a dick to other people. Don't be a dick to other people. Don't be a dick to other people. Don't be a dick to other people.

Don't be a dick to other people. Don't be a dick to other people. Don't be a dick to other people. Don't be a dick to other people. Don't be a dick to other people. Don't be a dick to other people. Don't be a dick to other people. Don't be a dick to other people. Don't be a dick to other people. Don't be a dick to other people. Don't be a dick to other people. Don't be a dick to other people. Don't be a dick to other people. Don't be a dick to other people. Don't be a dick

to other people. Don't be a
dick to other people. Don't
be a dick to other people.
Don't be a dick to other
people. Don't be a dick to
other people. Don't be a
dick to other people. Don't
be a dick to other people.
Don't be a dick to other
people. Don't be a dick to
other people. Don't be a
dick to other people. Don't
be a dick to other people.
Don't be a dick to other
people. Don't be a dick
to other people. Don't be
a dick to other people.
Don't be a dick to other

people. Don't be a dick to other people. Don't be a dick to other people. Don't be a dick to other people. Don't be a dick to other people. Don't be a dick to other people. Don't be a dick to other people. Don't be a dick to other people. Don't be a dick to other people. Don't be a dick to other people. Don't be a dick to other people. Don't be a dick to other people. Don't be a dick to other people. Don't be a dick to other people. Don't be a dick to other people. Don't be a dick to other people. Don't be a dick to other people. Don't be a dick to other people.

Don't be a dick to other people. Don't be a dick to other people. Don't be a dick to other people. Don't be a dick to other people. Don't be a dick to other people. Don't be a dick to other people. Don't be a dick to other people. Don't be a dick to other people. Don't be a dick to other people. Don't be a dick to other people. Don't be a dick to other people. Don't be a dick to other people. Don't be a dick to other people. Don't be a dick to other people. Don't be a dick

to other people. Don't be a dick to other people. Don't be a dick to other people. Don't be a dick to other people. Don't be a dick to other people. Don't be a dick to other people. Don't be a dick to other people. Don't be a dick to other people. Don't be a dick to other people. Don't be a dick to other people. Don't be a dick to other people. Don't be a dick to other people. Don't be a dick to other people. Don't be a dick to other people. Don't be a dick to other people. Don't be a dick to other people. Don't be a dick to other people. Don't be a dick to other

people. Don't be a dick to other people. Don't be a dick to other people. Don't be a dick to other people. Don't be a dick to other people. Don't be a dick to other people. Don't be a dick to other people. Don't be a dick to other people. Don't be a dick to other people. Don't be a dick to other people. Don't be a dick to other people. Don't be a dick to other people. Don't be a dick to other people. Don't be a dick to other people. Don't be a dick to other people. Don't be a dick to other people.

Don't be a dick to other people. Don't be a dick to other people. Don't be a dick to other people. Don't be a dick to other people. Don't be a dick to other people. Don't be a dick to other people. Don't be a dick to other people. Don't be a dick to other people. Don't be a dick to other people. Don't be a dick to other people. Don't be a dick to other people. Don't be a dick to other people. Don't be a dick to other people. Don't be a dick to other people. Don't be a dick

to other people. Don't be a
dick to other people. Don't
be a dick to other people.
Don't be a dick to other
people. Don't be a dick to
other people. Don't be a
dick to other people. Don't
be a dick to other people.
Don't be a dick to other
people. Don't be a dick to
other people. Don't be a
dick to other people. Don't
be a dick to other people.
Don't be a dick to other
people. Don't be a dick
to other people. Don't be
a dick to other people.
Don't be a dick to other

people. Don't be a dick to other people. Don't be a dick to other people. Don't be a dick to other people. Don't be a dick to other people. Don't be a dick to other people. Don't be a dick to other people. Don't be a dick to other people. Don't be a dick to other people. Don't be a dick to other people. Don't be a dick to other people. Don't be a dick to other people. Don't be a dick to other people. Don't be a dick to other people. Don't be a dick to other people. Don't be a dick to other people. Don't be a dick to other people.

Don't be a dick to other people. Don't be a dick to other people. Don't be a dick to other people. Don't be a dick to other people. Don't be a dick to other people. Don't be a dick to other people. Don't be a dick to other people. Don't be a dick to other people. Don't be a dick to other people. Don't be a dick to other people. Don't be a dick to other people. Don't be a dick to other people. Don't be a dick to other people. Don't be a dick

to other people. Don't be a
dick to other people. Don't
be a dick to other people.
Don't be a dick to other
people. Don't be a dick to
other people. Don't be a
dick to other people. Don't
be a dick to other people.
Don't be a dick to other
people. Don't be a dick to
other people. Don't be a
dick to other people. Don't
be a dick to other people.
Don't be a dick to other
people. Don't be a dick
to other people. Don't be
a dick to other people.
Don't be a dick to other

people. Don't be a dick to other people. Don't be a dick to other people. Don't be a dick to other people. Don't be a dick to other people. Don't be a dick to other people. Don't be a dick to other people. Don't be a dick to other people. Don't be a dick to other people. Don't be a dick to other people. Don't be a dick to other people. Don't be a dick to other people. Don't be a dick to other people. Don't be a dick to other people. Don't be a dick to other people. Don't be a dick to other people. Don't be a dick to other people.

Don't be a dick to other people. Don't be a dick to other people. Don't be a dick to other people. Don't be a dick to other people. Don't be a dick to other people. Don't be a dick to other people. Don't be a dick to other people. Don't be a dick to other people. Don't be a dick to other people. Don't be a dick to other people. Don't be a dick to other people. Don't be a dick to other people. Don't be a dick to other people. Don't be a dick to other people. Don't be a dick

to other people. Don't be a dick to other people. Don't be a dick to other people. Don't be a dick to other people. Don't be a dick to other people. Don't be a dick to other people. Don't be a dick to other people. Don't be a dick to other people. Don't be a dick to other people. Don't be a dick to other people. Don't be a dick to other people. Don't be a dick to other people. Don't be a dick to other people. Don't be a dick to other people. Don't be a dick to other people. Don't be a dick to other

people. Don't be a dick to other people. Don't be a dick to other people. Don't be a dick to other people. Don't be a dick to other people. Don't be a dick to other people. Don't be a dick to other people. Don't be a dick to other people. Don't be a dick to other people. Don't be a dick to other people. Don't be a dick to other people. Don't be a dick to other people. Don't be a dick to other people. Don't be a dick to other people. Don't be a dick to other people. Don't be a dick to other people. Don't be a dick to other people. Don't be a dick to other people. Don't be a dick to other people.

CONGRATULATIONS! Most people with a homophobia problem will have given up long before here.

So what have you learnt so far?

POP QUIZ!

① What should we not do to other people?

. . . .

② Who should we not be a dick to?

. . . .

By George I think you've got it!

Well done, you are well on your way to fighting not only your homophobia problem but a whole raft of other bigotries and anti-social ideas and behaviours.

Ok, now it's your turn, I'll get you started ...

Don't be a ....
....

Now keep going and fill up the rest of this book with your new mantra !!

Repeat after me:

Don't be a dick to other
people...

This time in capitals:

DON'T BE A DICK TO
OTHER PEOPLE...

Now in Comic Sans:

Don't be a dick to other people

This time in Portuguese:

Não seja um idiota com as outras pessoas

Freestyle . . .

You know what to do...

Keep going, you can make it...

Nearly there, just think of
all the new friends that
you'll make...

Come on! I believe in you!

Not far to go now...

3...

2 . . .

1 ...

Last one !!!

You're doing great. I know that it's hard but it's time for you to fly solo.

I know that it's scary but keep going, you're doing so well.

Work everyday to make the world a better place and remember:

Don't be a dick to other people!

Sophie Cook

⭐

@sophiecooktalks

Printed in Great Britain
by Amazon